First
1000 Words

How to use this book

Small children love looking at pictures and naming what they see. It can be even more fun if they share a word book with a grown-up. You could start by talking about what is going on in the big pictures. There will be many things that your child will recognize, as well as new objects to discuss.

On pages with small pictures around the edge, children will enjoy finding each image in the large picture. It is useful to talk about the colors and shapes they are looking for, as the scale of the object may be very different in each place.

Rhymes at the bottom of each page encourage children to look more closely at the pictures and to talk about their own experience. Finally, they are asked to find Teddy Bear (who appears on the cover of this book) wherever he is hiding!

As children gain confidence, they will enjoy finding objects throughout the book, not simply on one page. Later still, you could introduce them to the Word List at the back, showing them that it is organized alphabetically.

One of the best ways to help your child to enjoy books and reading is to show that you enjoy them too. We hope you both have fun with this book!

Teddy Bear's
Fun to Learn

First
1000 Words

Written by Nicola Baxter

Illustrated by Susie Lacome

ARMADILLO

This edition produced in 2006 for MJF Media
by arrangement with Armadillo Books
an imprint of Bookmart Limited
Registered Number 2372865
Trading as Bookmart Limited
Blaby Road, Wigston, Leicestershire, LE18 4SE

ISBN 1-90046-581-7

3 5 7 9 10 8 6 4 2

Produced for Bookmart Limited by
Nicola Baxter
PO Box 215, Framingham Earl,
Norwich NR14 7UR

Editorial consultant: Ronne Randall
Designer: Amanda Hawkes

Printed in Singapore

Contents

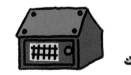

At Home

trash can　　pail　　tool box　　window bo[x]

roof

pipe

path

chimney

ladder

window

door

Uncle Ted is working hard,
Fixing a loose tile.
What might he be listening to
That brings a happy smile?

radio

doorstep

thermos flask

lunch box

bricks

roof tile

trellis

security light

driveway

doorbell

napkin

antenna

glove

Can you see two yellow gloves
For Uncle Ted to wear?
What is in his tool box?
And where's that Teddy Bear?

The Kitchen

jug saucepan cookbook toaster

rolling pin

storage jar

fridge

wooden spoon

frying pan

tea towel

microwave

Someone's busy helping
His mommy cook a cake.
Can you see how big a mess
A little bear can make?

 shelf

 stool

 oven

 kettle

 iron

 sink

 blender

 dishwashing liquid

 drawer

 cork board

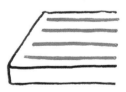 dishwasher

 draining board

 mixing bowl

Where is the saucepan lid?
How many spoons are there?
What is in the open drawer?
And where is Teddy Bear?

The Bedroom

hairbrush   duvet   mobile   comb

bed

closet

chest of drawers

bedside table

pyjamas

bathrobe

pillow

Here is Teddy's bedroom
And Teddy's little bed.
How many things
Can you see that are red?

slippers

socks

toy box

poster

kite

comic

light

height chart

wastepaper basket

alarm clock

painting

coathanger

piggy bank

Can you find both Teddy's socks
To make a perfect pair?
What's that on his duvet?
And where is Teddy Bear?

11

The Bathroom

soap   wash cloth   sponge   toothbrush

bath

wash stand

toilet paper

shower

shower curtain

bath mat

cabinet

When a bear's been doing painting
He's never very clean.
If you follow colored pawprints
You can see just where he's been.

toilet   mirror   nail brush   tap   scales   towel

shampoo

bubble bath

toothpaste

toy boat

wall tiles

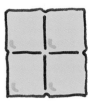

back brush

rubber duck

Yes, Teddy Bear's left pawprints
Almost everywhere.
Can you see a purple print?
And where is Teddy Bear?

The Living Room

clock   curtain   lamp   cushic

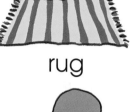

rug

armchair

bookcase

magazine

vacuum cleaner

plant

dust cloth

Someone's being busy
Cleaning up the living room.
Can you see three dust cloths
And the end of a broom?

newspaper   vase   VCR/DVD player   photograph   carpet   picture   table

remote control

sofa

fireplace

television

stereo

wallpaper

How many flowers
In the vase are there?
What's in the fireplace?
And where is Teddy Bear?

The Attic

cradle

doll house

cage

skylight

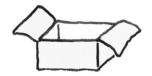
cardboard box

picture frame

suitcase

dressmaker's
dummy

skis

light bulb

spider's web

There may be treasures in the attic
As every teddy knows.
What can you see that would
Be useful when it snows?

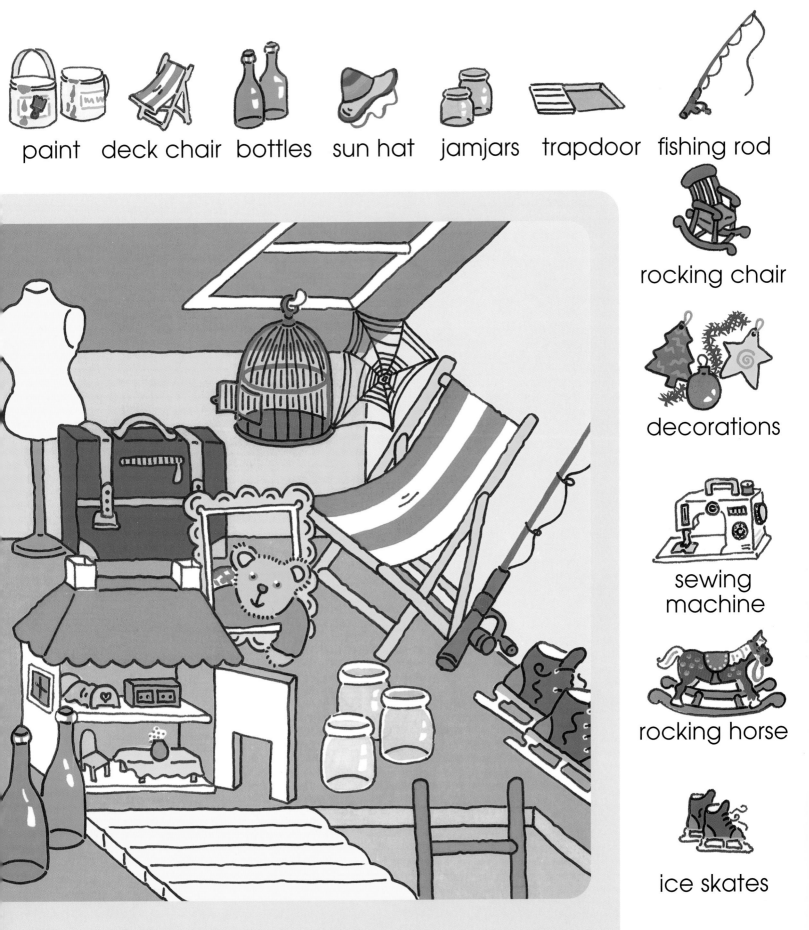

paint deck chair bottles sun hat jamjars trapdoor fishing rod

rocking chair

decorations

sewing machine

rocking horse

ice skates

sled

And what could you use
When the sun is shining bright?
Can you count the jamjars?
And is Teddy Bear in sight?

The Garden

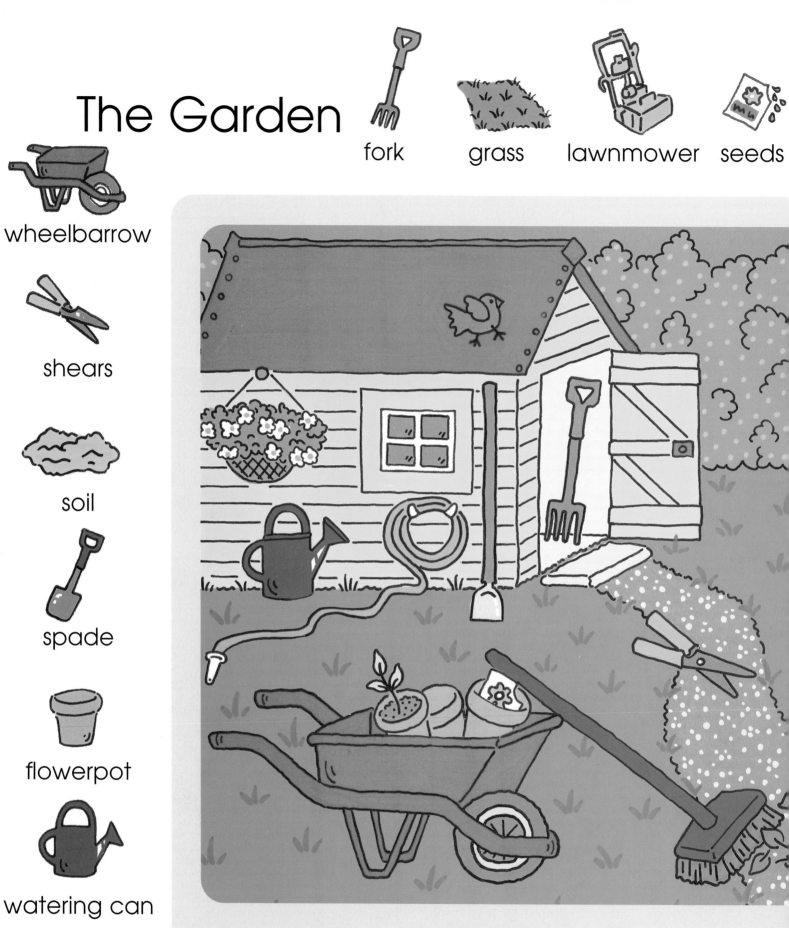

fork

grass

lawnmower

seeds

wheelbarrow

shears

soil

spade

flowerpot

watering can

hose

In this lovely garden
Many plants and flowers grow.
But what comes tumbling from the tree
When strong winds blow?

leaves

bird house

hoe

hand fork

hand shovel

bird table

shed

hanging basket

rake

hedge

flowers

bird bath

broom

After hard work in the sunshine,
The garden looks its best.
Can you spot that Teddy Bear
Taking a well-earned rest?

The Street

bicycle

pigeon

candy jar

cake

sidewalk

railings

street light

trash can

delivery van

driver

stroller

The street is always busy.
How many bears can you spy?
Have you noticed anything
That **you** would like to buy?

school　　bakery　　parcel　　road　　sucker　　drain　　safety helmet

shopping bag

shoe store

High Street

street sign

candy store

skipping rope

boots

High Street

Where could you find some slippers?
Where could you buy a bun?
Can you see that Teddy Bear
Having lots of fun?

The Supermarket

change purse   money   fruit   purse

cans

shopper

shopping cart

line-up

shopping basket

grocery bag

cash register

Teddy Bear loves shopping.
Do you like it too?
How many shoppers are
standing in the line-up?

milk
 keys
 yoghurt
 carton
 juice
 honey
 barcode

 store clerk

 till receipt

 sign

 cashier

 vegetables

 conveyor belt

How many teddies
Wearing blue are there?
Can you find the carrots?
Can you see that Teddy Bear?

23

At School

teacher　markers　paper　water pot

ruler

chalkboard

map

crayons

modelling clay

chalk

coat hooks

There's so much to do
At Teddy's nursery school.
But coming in late
Is not the rule!

pupil   paintbrush   eraser   portrait   aquarium   easel   paintbox

alphabet

notebook

computer

backpack

puzzle

scissors

a b c d e
f g h i j k l
m n o p q
r s t u v w
x y z

How many girls
Have bows in their hair?
Who's making pawprints?
And where's that Teddy Bear?

25

On the Move

helicopter

balloon

rocket

parachute

coach

car

tow truck

motor home

mini van

dump truck

vintage car

two-seater
bicycle

bulldozer

How many wheels
Can you see here?
Which of the vehicles
Would be hardest to steer?

racing car

steamroller

garbage truck

transport truck

go-kart

truck

motorbike

tanker

backhoe

car transporter

moving van

Which vehicle is the oldest?
(It's really very rare.)
Which could travel farthest?
And where's that Teddy Bear?

The Farm

sheep   lamb   pig   piglet

chicks

hen

dog

horse

foal

farmer

farmhouse

Here's a busy farmer.
What's that in his hand?
Can you name the animals
That live on his land?

duck   duckling   cat   mouse   gate   fence   scarecrow

pond

rooster

cow

calf

field

Who's in the duck pond?
How many chicks are there?
Who's that rolling in the mud?
And where is Teddy Bear?

tractor

The Park

 bench knee pads bird horn

ice cream

slide

swing

jogger

sand box

fountain

flower bed

In the park one sunny day
Teddy bears are having fun.
How many are there?
Can you count them, one by one?

tricycle skateboard teeter totter wheels hamper hoop ball

picnic

squirrel

sandwiches

scooter

rollerskates

CD player

How many bears
On wheels are there?
What is in the hamper?
And where is Teddy Bear?

Storybook World

wand

wishing well   toadstool   elf   fairy

lance   shield   crown

sword

armor

dragon   knight princess

Can you tell a story
About everything you see?
Who can do **real** magic?
Who is brave as he can be?

banner

top hat

page

pumpkin

magician

prince   queen   king   giant   castle

cloak

Do you know the names for clothes
That knights and princes wear?
Who lost a glass slipper?
Can you spot our Teddy Bear?

The Countryside

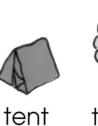 tent   tree   hiker   bridge

forest

mountain

meadow

river

lake

branch

camp fire

The countryside is beautiful,
A lovely place to be.
How many green things
Can you see?

trunk   engine   carriage   bush   binoculars   waterfall   log

village

railway track

rowboat

hill

sleeping bag

Can you count two flowers?
Can you see a little train?
Does the village have a church?
Find Teddy Bear again!

rocks

The Harbor

fish   paddles   rope   buoy

portholes

submarine

liner

fisherman

crane

fishing boat

motor boat

Here's a busy harbor.
Which is your favorite boat?
Which things are meant to sink
And which are meant to float?

life vest hook anchor lobster mast canoe water-skier

lobster trap

wetsuit

jetty

container ship

diver

life ring

The back of a boat is called the stern.
The front is called the bow.
Our Teddy's holding paddles.
Can you see him now?

The Airport

toilets　　hangar　　label　　clipboard

walking stick

milkshake

baggage trolley

arrivals board

airport bus

airplane

control tower

At this busy airport,
Travelling teddies come and go.
Where's the public telephone?
What does a pilot do?

briefcase coffee runway broom cleaner tickets camera

windsock

pilot

check-in

stewardess

backpack

telephone

Is the weather very windy?
Who keeps the airport clean?
And is our little Teddy Bear
Anywhere to be seen?

The Hospital

tray

nurse

water

bandage

sheet

doctor

nightgown

medicine

visitor

walker

cotton balls

When a teddy's feeling poorly
Or has had a nasty fall,
She'll get better in the hospital
In no time at all.

elevator

porter

watch

sling

adhesive
bandage

syringe

blanket

get-well card

cast

temperature
chart

stethoscope

thermometer

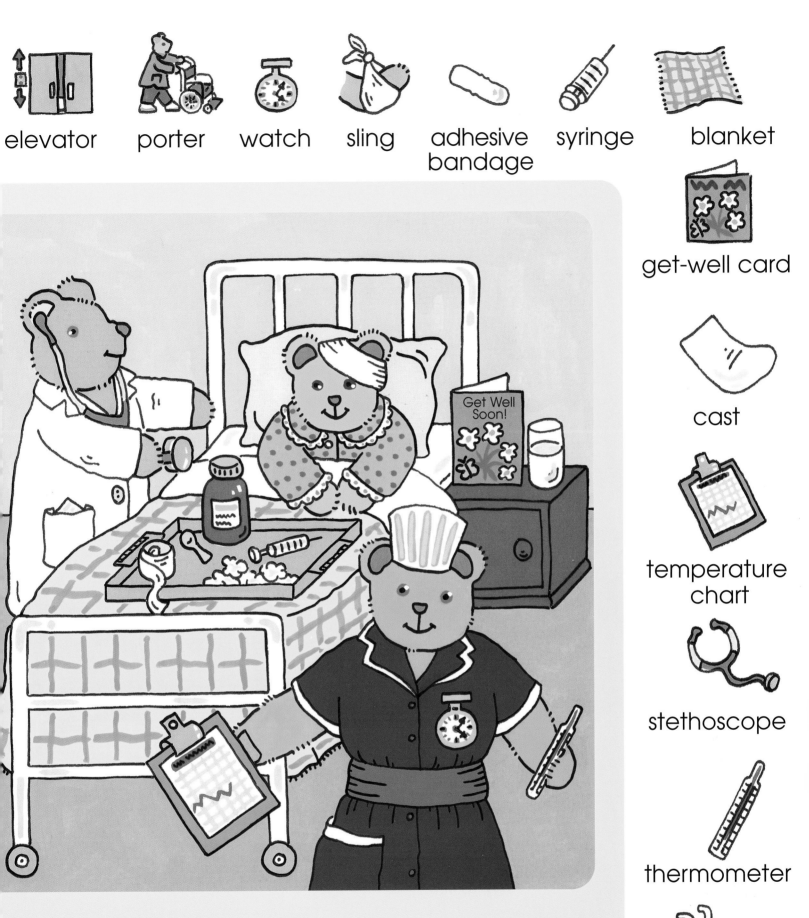

wheelchair

Can you see a visitor
With presents for sick bears?
And can you spot our Teddy Bear,
Who didn't climb the stairs?

All at Sea

 pirate flag  seahorse   chain   pearl

 whale

 pirate ship

 message in a bottle

 shark

swimmer

treasure chest

 jellyfish

Ahoy there, teddy bears!
What treasures can you spy,
Down at the bottom of the sea,
Where the jellyfish floats by?

coral

octopus

pirate

dolphin

pistol

eye patch

oyster

treasure map

keyhole

island

seaweed

mermaid

palm tree

What is on the pirate flag?
How many shells can you see?
Who has got the treasure map?
And where can Teddy Bear be?

The Toy Shop

 abacus  skittles  fort  doll

tea set

Jack-in-the-box

pencil crayons

top

play house

board game

puppet

Teddy loves the toy shop.
It's a super place to play.
Which toy would you like to have
If you could choose today?

44

beads

wagon

yo-yo

dice

marbles

robot

stacking cups

building bricks

pull-along toy

soldiers

coloring book

pedal car

dress up clothes

How can the shopkeeper
Reach the highest shelf?
And where has little Teddy Bear
Hidden himself?

The Workshop

wrench **flashlight** **mug** **drill**

pocket

calendar

shelf

doorknob

measuring tape

cookies

Noah's ark

Someone's helping Uncle Ted
To make a Noah's Ark.
Which tool would be useful
For seeing in the dark?

 saw   screwdriver   screws   nails    hammer   goggles   penknife

sandpaper

mallet

plank

animals

pliers

workbench

What is our teddy holding?
What are those goggles for?
Which other animals could Ted make?
What color is the door?

47

The Seaside

 flag  sand  sea shell sea

sandcastle

starfish

swimsuit

umbrella

pebbles

fishing net

sunglasses

It's lovely at the seaside
With sun and sand and sea.
What are these teddies doing?
How many can you see?

48

 crab

 flippers

 yacht

 water wings

 sun

 waves

 sun screen

 lighthouse

 rubber ring

 beachball

 bathing suit

 sea gull

 popsicle

How do the bears make extra sure
They're not burnt by the sun?
How many sea shells can you see?
Where's our Teddy having fun?

Party Time

present

clown

candle

button

straw

party hat

slice of cake

pop

paper cup

tablecloth

birthday cake

Happy Birthday, Teddy Tim!
How old are your today?
Lots of friends have come to share
Your very special day.

50

vest ribbon balloon bow tie mask bow blindfold

wrapping paper

streamers

party bag

envelope

birthday card

party dress

How many bears are wearing hats?
How many presents are there?
How many balls are in the air?
Can you spot our Teddy Bear?

Parts of the Body

eyebrow

hair

thumb

hand

palm

lip

cheek

elbow

knee

wrist

finger

ankle

toe

Can you count Dolly's fingers?
Can you count her toes?
Can you put **your** finger
On her little button nose?

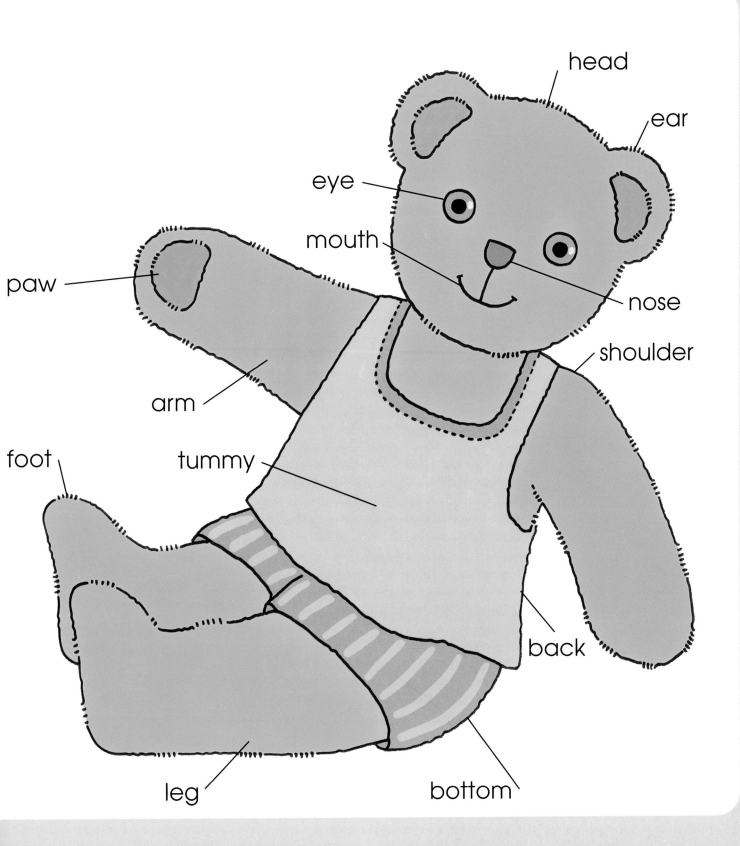

head

ear

eye

mouth

nose

shoulder

paw

arm

foot

tummy

back

leg

bottom

Dolly's eyes are brightest brown.
Teddy's eyes are blue.
What color are **your** lovely eyes?
Can you name each part of **you**?

Busy Teddies

crawling

sitting

reading

cuddling

singing

drinking

eating

writing

waving

washing

drying

sleeping

What a lot of busy teddies!
Can you copy what they do?
What is one teddy eating?
Who is using pink shampoo?

| kicking | jumping | riding | hopping |

| walking | dressing | running | skipping |

| pushing | pulling | dancing | standing |

What is the standing teddy holding?
Who needs another sock to wear?
What do you need for skipping?
Can you see that Teddy Bear?

Seasons

spring

summer

autumn

winter

The year is always changing.
Which season is it now?
Our bear has fun the whole year through,
Can you tell me how?

Weather

sunshine

snow

rainbow

ice

hurricane

icicles

wind

snowflake

cloud

tornado

snowman

rain

dew

lightning

hot

flood

frost

fog

cold

puddles

Look out of the window.
What's the weather like today?
What kind of weather is the best
For going out to play?

Favorite Food

butter

biscuit

cereal

sugar

soup

hotdog

fries

sauces

chocolate

rice

doughnuts

spaghetti

Here are Teddy's favorite foods.
What do you like to eat?
Which of these foods are savory
And which of them are sweet?

salad

hamburger

pizza

baked beans

muffin

cheese

bread

sausages

nuts

flour

omelette

pie

Can you see what happens
When Teddy helps to bake?
When you help in the kitchen
What do you like to make?

Sports and Games

cricket

baseball

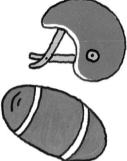
football

tennis

high jump

archery

three-legged race

climbing

diving

pole vaulting

team

gymnastics

Here are lots of teddies!
Have you tried these sports?
How many bears are jumping high?
Which ones are wearing shorts?

ampolining	cycling	weightlifting	rowing

roller skating	golf	soccer	sack race

ice skating	basketball	martial arts	trophy

Why might you get a trophy?
Does it matter if you win?
Which teddy has a target?
Which race is Teddy Bear in?

Music, Please!

tambourine

triangle

cymbals

maracas

violin

keyboard

trombone

recorder

music stand

notes

conductor

cello

Can you play an instrument?
Do you like to dance and sing?
Which instruments go toot-de-toot?
And which goes ting-a-ling?

flute   music   oboe   trumpet

axophone   banjo   xylophone   guitar

harp   piano   timpani

Which instruments do you have to blow?
Which ones do you bang or shake?
Do you know what a conductor does?
What difference does he make?

Baby Bears

rattle   bib   baby bottle   soother

bootees

baby monitor

changing mat

baby record book

money box

sleeper

crib

Twin babies keep you busy!
Teddy's helping out today.
Where is one baby's cuddly toy?
What is she throwing away?

buggy shawl diaper tissues teething ring potty high chair

trainer cup

cloth book

board book

cuddly toy

mattress

changing bag

Why do babies sleep in special beds
And sit in special chairs?
Can you remember when you were
As small as these baby bears?

Numbers

one house

two cars

three kites

four rabbits

five balloons

six ducks

seven strawberries

eight crayons

nine flowers

ten hearts

Can you count from one to ten?
How many flowers can you see?
Can you count from ten to one?
How many kites are flying free?

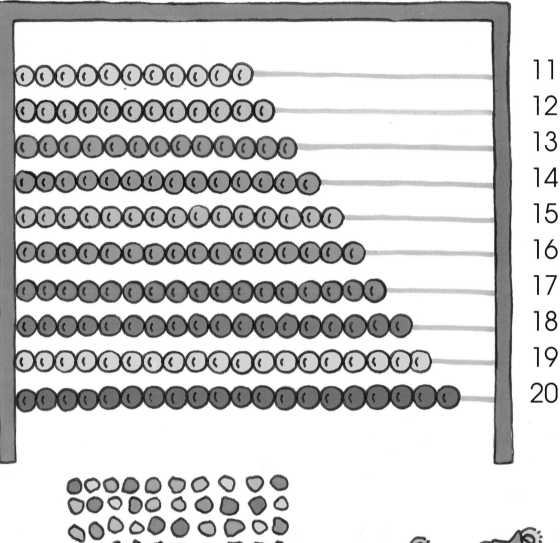

11 eleven
12 twelve
13 thirteen
14 fourteen
15 fifteen
16 sixteen
17 seventeen
18 eighteen
19 nineteen
20 twenty

100 one hundred

third   second   first

How many beads are colored green?
How many are colored blue?
Will our Teddy win his race?
Can you count to one hundred too?

Colors

 blue red grey  pink  green

white

black

yellow

brown

purple

orange

navy

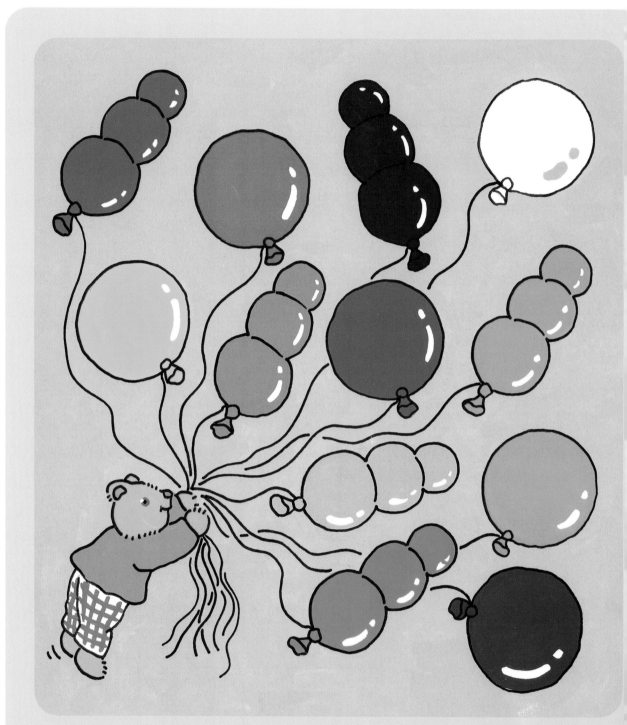

Look at all the big balloons
That Teddy's holding tight!
Which is your favorite color?
Is it pale or is it bright?

Shapes

heart · stripes · circle · square · star · diamond

rectangle

zigzags

spots

oval

triangle

checkers

Teddy's painted lots of shapes
With patterns in between.
What has Teddy painted red?
Which shape is colored green?

Clothes

 hat    handkerchief   mittens    running shoes

scarf

jeans

jacket

blouse

undershirt

pants

sweater

Teddy's hanging lots of clothes
On the line to dry.
Who do you think helped
To peg the rest so high?

winter jacket
boots shorts
skirt
underwear
T-shirt
clothes pin
shoes
overalls
shirt
coat
tie
tights

Which clothes might be Teddy's own?
Which would you like to wear?
Have you got as many clothes
As lucky Teddy Bear?

Families

great grandmother   great grandfather

grandmother   grandfather   great aunt   great uncle

father   mother   aunt   uncle

sister   Teddy Bear   brother   cousin   twins

Here is Teddy's family.
He's waving – can you see?
Who are all the people
On your family tree?

Feelings

frightened

happy

shy

embarrassed

bored

angry

thoughtful

sad

proud

sorry

How are these teddies feeling?
What has made a teddy cry?
Why is another sorry?
Have you ever felt shy?

Fruits

raspberry

grapes

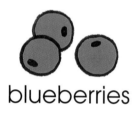
blueberries

fig

mango

rhubarb

gooseberry

pear

banana

melon

lime

The bowl is full of juicy fruit!
What would you choose to eat?
Which fruits can taste a little sharp
And which are always sweet?

74

orange
 peach
 lemon
 plum
 apricot
 cherry
 apple

 papaya

 grapefruit

 strawberry

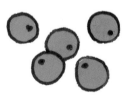 redcurrants

 tangerine

 pineapple

Can you always eat the skin?
How many strawberries are there?
Which fruit is just about to be
Eaten by Teddy Bear?

75

Vegetables

mushrooms

carrot

broccoli

red pepper

peas

leek

sweetcorn

onion

potato

cauliflower

tomatoes

celery

Vegetables are good to eat.
Which ones have you tasted?
What is Teddy munching,
Making sure that none is wasted?

 lettuce

 beetroot

 broad beans

 parsnip

 cucumber

 radishes

 sweet potato

 string beans

 turnip

 herbs

 cabbage

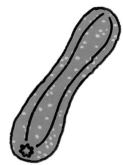 zucchini

Which vegetables need to be cooked?
Which ones can you eat raw?
Which do you like to eat so much
You always ask for more?

Flowers

 poppy   iris    daisy   bluebell

pansy

daffodil

dahlia

sunflower

carnation

lily

rose

Which flowers are yellow?
Which flowers are blue?
And which can grow
Even taller than you?

78

Time to Eat!

teaspoon pepper salt saucer cup

plate

knife

fork

spoon

tablemat

glass

water jug

Teddy is setting the table.
What is he holding up?
And what do you often find
Underneath a cup?

Opposites

slow

fast

big

little

tall

short

open

shut

on

off

bottom

top

Are you bigger than an elephant?
Are you smaller than a mouse?
Do you go to sleep at night
Outside or inside your house?

up

down

old

new

full

empty

light

heavy

inside

outside

thin

fat

Are you young or are you old?
Are you a girl or boy?
And can you see that Teddy Bear
With a favorite toy?

Birds

egg

beak

wing

feather

nest

owl

puffin

toucan

penguin

peacock

ostrich

emu

Do you know which of these birds
Never fly at all?
Which ones love to eat a fish?
Which one is very tall?

kingfisher   swallow   kiwi   hummingbird

albatross   vulture   goose   turkey

flamingo   pelican   stork   swan

What noise does a turkey make?
What about an owl?
Can you see where Teddy Bear
Is feeding a waterfowl?

Minibeasts

bee

snail

ladybug

lizard

worm

butterfly

wasp

caterpillar

beetle

millipede

chameleon

Which minibeasts can creep or crawl?
Which ones hop or fly?
Which ones can be hard to see
If you walk quickly by?

moth

 ant

 grasshopper

 slug

 fly

 flea

chrysalis

stick insect

tarantula

frog

centipede

dragonfly

spider

Which minibeasts can sting or bite?
Why do you think they do?
And can you spot that Teddy Bear
Watching them – and you?

Wild Animals

koala

rhinoceros

armadillo

kangaroo

polar bear

gorilla

giraffe

monkey

tiger

elephant

snake

panda

Can you see an animal
Who goes along by jumping?
Can you see another one
Who gives his chest a thumping?

| raccoon | buffalo | porcupine | zebra |

| bear | crocodile | camel | lion |

| wolf | leopard | beaver | hippopotamus |

Who has lots of prickles?
Who lives in a lair?
And who is being fed
By a kindly Teddy Bear?

Animal Friends

kennel   kitten   hamster   animal cage

canary

rabbit

parrot

budgie

guinea pig

petfood

goldfish

Who lives in a kennel?
Who has a special door?
What color is the parrot?
What is that small brush for?

puppy   bubbles   brush   tortoise   bone   leash   collar

dog bowl

cat basket

fish tank

cat flap

turtle

How many bubbles
In the fish tank are there?
And what tasty rabbit snack
Is being held by Teddy Bear?

water bowl

89

Word List

a

abacus	44
adhesive bandage	41
airplane	38
airport bus	38
alarm clock	11
albatross	83
alphabet	25
anchor	37
angry	73
animal cage	88
animals	47
ankle	52
ant	85
antenna	7
apple	75
apricot	75
aquarium	25
archery	60
arm	53
armadillo	86
armchair	14
armor	32
arrivals board	38
aunt	72
autumn	56

b

baby bottle	64
baby monitor	64
baby record book	64
back	53
back brush	13
backhoe	27
backpack	25
backpack	39

baggage trolley	38
baked beans	59
bakery	21
ball	31
balloon	51
banana	74
bandage	40
banjo	63
banner	33
barcode	23
baseball	60
basket	11
basketball	61
bath	12
bath mat	12
bath robe	10
bathing suit	49
beachball	49
beads	45
beak	82
bear	87
beaver	87
bed	10
bedside table	10
bee	84
beetle	84
beetroot	77
bench	30
bib	64
bicycle	20
big	80
binoculars	35
bird	30
bird bath	19
bird house	19
bird table	19
birthday cake	50
birthday card	51
biscuit	58
black	68

blanket	41
blender	9
blindfold	51
blouse	70
blue	68
bluebell	78
blueberries	74
board book	65
board game	44
bone	89
bookcase	14
bootees	64
boots	21
boots	71
bored	73
bottles	17
bottom	53
bottom	80
bow	51
bow tie	51
branch	34
bread	59
bricks	7
bridge	34
briefcase	39
broad beans	77
broccoli	76
broom	19
brother	72
brown	68
brush	89
bubble bath	13
bubbles	89
budgie	88
buffalo	87
buggy	65
bulldozer	26
buoy	36
bush	35
butter	58

butterfly	84
button	50

c

cabbage	77
cabinet	12
cage	16
cake	20
calendar	46
calf	29
camel	87
camera	39
camp fire	34
canary	88
candle	50
candy jar	20
candy store	21
canoe	37
cans	22
car	26
cardboard box	16
carnation	78
carpet	15
carriage	35
carrot	76
car transporter	27
carton	23
cashier	23
cash register	22
cast	41
castle	33
cat	29
cat basket	89
cat flap	89
caterpillar	84
cauliflower	76
CD player	31
celery	76
cello	62

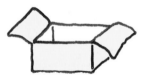

peacock	82	pole vaulting	60	radio	7	rug	14
pear	74	pond	29	radishes	77	ruler	24
pearl	42	pop	50	railings	20	running	55
peas	76	popsicle	49	railway track	35	running shoes	70
pebbles	48	poppy	78	rain	57	runway	39
pedal car	45	porcupine	87	rainbow	57		
pelican	83	porter	41	rake	19	**s**	
pencil crayons	44	portholes	36	raspberry	74		
penguin	82	portrait	25	rattle	64	sack race	61
penknife	47	poster	11	reading	54	sad	73
pepper	79	potato	76	recorder	62	safety helmet	21
petfood	88	potty	65	rectangle	69	salad	59
photograph	15	present	50	red	68	salt	79
piano	63	prince	32	red pepper	76	sand	48
picnic	31	princess	32	redcurrants	75	sand box	30
picture	15	proud	73	remote control	15	sandcastle	48
picture frame	16	puddles	57	rhinoceros	86	sandpaper	47
pie	59	puffin	82	rhubarb	74	sandwiches	31
pig	28	pull-along toy	45	ribbon	51	saucepan	8
pigeon	20	pulling	55	rice	58	saucer	79
piggy bank	11	pumpkin	33	riding	55	sauces	58
piglet	28	pupil	25	river	34	sausages	59
pillow	10	puppet	44	road	21	saw	47
pilot	39	puppy	89	robot	45	saxophone	63
pineapple	75	purple	68	rocket	26	scales	13
pink	68	purse	22	rocking chair	17	scarecrow	29
pipe	6	pushing	55	rocking horse	17	scarf	70
pirate	43	puzzle	25	rocks	35	school	21
pirate flag	42	pyjamas	10	roller skating	61	scissors	25
pirate ship	42			rollerskates	31	scooter	31
pistol	43			rolling pin	8	screwdriver	47
pizza	59	**q**		roof	6	screws	47
plank	47	queen	33	roof tile	7	sea	48
plant	14			rooster	29	sea gull	49
plate	79			rope	36	seahorse	42
play house	44	**r**		rose	78	sea shell	48
pliers	47			rowboat	35	seaweed	43
plum	75	rabbit	88	rowing	61	second	67
pocket	46	raccoon	87	rubber duck	13	security light	7
polar bear	86	racing car	27	rubber ring	49	seeds	18

95

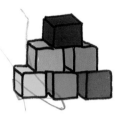